SCIENCE PROJECTS

Plants

Patricia Whitehouse

www.heinemann.co.uk/library
Visit our website to find out more information about Heinemann Library books.

To order:
☎ Phone 44 (0)1865 888066
▤ Send a fax to 44 (0)1865 314091
▭ Visit the Heinemann Library Bookshop at www.heinemann.co.uk/library to browse our catalogue and order online.

First published in Great Britain by Heinemann Library, Halley Court, Jordan Hill, Oxford OX2 8EJ, part of Pearson Education. Heinemann Library is a registered trademark of Pearson Education Ltd.

Produced for Pearson Education by White-Thomson Publishing Ltd. Bridgewater Business Centre, 210 High Street, Lewes, East Sussex BN7 2NH

Editorial: Brian Fitzgerald
Design: Tim Mayer and Alison Walper
Illustrations: Cavedweller Studio
Picture Research: Amy Sparks
Production: Duncan Gilbert

Originated by Modern Age
Printed and bound in China by Leo Paper Group

ISBN 978 0 431 04042 4 (hardback)
12 11 10 09 08
10 9 8 7 6 5 4 3 2 1

ISBN 978 0 431 04049 3 (paperback)
12 11 10 09 08
10 9 8 7 6 5 4 3 2 1

British Library Cataloguing in Publication Data
Whitehouse, Patricia, 1958-
Plants. – (Science projects)
580
A full catalogue record for this book is available from the British Library.

Acknowledgements
The author and publishers are grateful to the following for permission to reproduce copyright material: AGStockUSA, Inc./Alamy **p. 24**; Corbis, Masterfile **p. 4** (Andrew Douglas), **36** (George H. H. Huey); iStockphoto.com, **title page, pp. 20, 12** (Hazel Proudlove), **16** (Arpad Benedek), **28** (Guy Erwood); Photolibrary **pp. 8** (OSF), **32** (Mark Bolton), **40** (Photononstop)

Cover photograph reproduced with permission of istockphoto.com.

The publishers would like to thank Sue Glass for her assistance in the preparation of this book.

Every effort has been made to contact copyright holders of any material reproduced in this book. Any omissions will be rectified in subsequent printings if notice is given to the publishers.

Contents

» Any words appearing in bold, **like this,**
are explained in the glossary.

Starting your science investigation

A science investigation is an exciting challenge. It starts with an idea that you can test by doing experiments. These are often lots of fun to do. But it is no good just charging in without planning first. A good scientist knows that they must first research their idea thoroughly, work out how they can test it, and plan their experiments carefully. When they have done these things, they can happily carry out their experiments to see if their idea is right.

Your experiments might support your original idea or they might shoot it down in flames. This doesn't matter. The important thing is that you will have found out a bit more about the world around you, and had fun along the way. You will be a happy scientist!

In this book, you'll look at nine science investigations involving plants. You'll be able to discover some wonderful things about the world you live in.

Do your research

Is there something about plants that you've always wondered about? Something you don't quite understand but would like to? Then do a little research about the subject. Go to the library and find some books about the subject. Books written for students are often a very good place to start.

Use your favourite Internet search engine to find reliable online resources. Websites written by museums, universities, newspapers, and scientific journals are among the best sources for **accurate** research. Each investigation in this book has some suggestions for further research.

You need to make sure that your resources are reliable when doing research. Ask yourself the following questions, especially about the resources you find online.

The investigations Background information

The start of each investigation contains a box like this.

Possible question

This question is a suggested starting point for your investigation. You will need to adapt the question to suit the things that interest you.

Possible hypothesis

This is only a suggestion. Don't worry if your hypothesis doesn't match the one listed here. Use your imagination!

Approximate cost of materials

Discuss this with your parents before starting work. Don't spend too much.

Materials needed

Make sure you can easily get all of the materials listed and gather them together before starting work.

Level of difficulty

There are three levels of investigations in this book: Easy, Intermediate, and Advanced. The level of difficulty is based on how long the investigation takes and how complicated it is.

1) How old is the resource? Is the information up to date or is it very old?

2) Who wrote the resource? Is the author identified so you know who they are, and what qualifies them to write about the topic?

3) What is the purpose of the resource? A website from a business or pressure group might not give balanced information, but one from a university probably will.

4) Is the information well documented? Can you tell where the author got their information from so you can check how accurate it is?

Some websites allow you to "chat" online with experts. Make sure you discuss this with a parent or teacher first. Never give out personal information online. The "Think U Know" website at http://www.thinkuknow.co.uk has loads of tips about safety online.

Once you know a little more about the subject you want to investigate, you'll be ready to work out your scientific question. You will be able to use this to make a sensible **hypothesis**. A hypothesis is an idea about why something happens that can be tested by doing experiments. Finally, you'll be ready to begin your science investigation!

Plants are a great subject for science investigations. Plants are inexpensive and easy to maintain. They react in interesting ways to light, temperature, and gravity.

What is an experiment?

Often when someone says that they are going to do an experiment, they mean they are just going to fiddle with something to see what happens. But scientists mean something else. They mean that they are going to control the **variables** involved in a careful way. A variable is something that changes or can be changed. Independent variables are things that you deliberately keep the same or change in your experiment. You should always aim to keep all the independent variables constant, except for the one you are investigating. The dependent variable is the change that happens because of the one independent variable that you do change. You make a fair test if you set up your experiment so that you only change one independent variable at a time. Your results are valid if you have carried out a fair test, and recorded your results or observations honestly.

Sometimes you might want to compare one group with another to see what happens. For example, if you wanted to show the effect of minerals on plants, you might use 10 potted plants. You would give five of them tap water only (Group A) and five of them liquid fertiliser (Group B). Group A is your **control** group and group B is your test group. You would be looking to see if there is a difference between the two groups. In this experiment, the liquid fertiliser is the independent variable, and the effect on the plant is the dependent variable.

You must do experiments carefully so that your results are accurate and reliable. Ideally, you would get the same results if you did your investigation all over again.

Your hypothesis

Once you've decided on the question you're going to try to answer, you then make a scientific **prediction** of what you'll find out in your science project.

For example, if you notice that plants don't grow much in the winter, your question might be, "Does temperature affect how fast plants grow?". Remember, a hypothesis is an idea about why something happens, which can be tested by doing experiments. So your hypothesis in response to the above question might be, "Plants grow more slowly at lower temperatures". With a hypothesis, you can also work out if you can actually do the experiments needed to answer your question. Think of a question like: "How many seeds are there in the world?". It would be impossible to support your hypothesis, however you express it. This is because you can't possibly count all of the seeds in the world. So, be sure you can actually get the **evidence** needed to support or disprove your hypothesis.

Keeping records

Good scientists keep careful notes in their lab book about everything they do. This is really important. Other scientists may want to try out the experiments to see if they get the same results. So the records in your lab book need to be clear and easy to follow. What sort of things should you write down?

It is a good idea to write some notes about the research you found in books and on websites. You should also include the names of the books or the web addresses. This will save you from having to find these useful resources all over again later. You should also write down your hypothesis and your reasons for it. All your **data** and results should go into your lab book, too.

Your results are the evidence that you use to make your conclusion. Never rub out an odd-looking result or tweak it to "look right". An odd result may turn out to be important later. You should write down *every* result you get. Tables are a really good way to record lots of results clearly. Make sure you record when you did your experiments, and anything you might have changed along the way to improve them. No detail is too small when it comes to scientific research.

There are tips for making a great report with each investigation and at the end of this book. Use them as guides and don't be afraid to be creative. Make it *your* investigation!

Seeds and gravity

Seeds are the beginning of life for many plants. When the seeds are in the ground, how do they know which way to grow? Do the stems always grow up, and do the roots always grow down? Does it make a difference whether the seeds are planted the right way up or upside down? This experiment will help you find out.

Do your research

Plants can grow or bend as a reaction to changes in their environment. The responses are called **tropisms.** Before you begin this project, do some research on plants and **geotropism,** a plant's reaction to gravity. Once you've done some research, you can dig into this project. Or, you may come up with your own unique project after you've read and learned more about the topic.

Here are some books and websites you could start with in your research:

» *The Green World: Plant Development*, William G Hopkins (Chelsea House, 2006)

Background information

Possible question

Does the direction in which you plant a seed affect the direction it grows?

Possible hypothesis

The direction in which you plant a seed does not affect the direction of growth.

Level of difficulty

Intermediate

Approximate cost of materials

£4.00

Materials needed

» Eight sunflower seeds (the type used for planting, not for eating)
» Plastic cup
» Two re-sealable sandwich bags
» Cotton wool balls
» Water
» Drawing pin
» Permanent marker
» Sticky tape
» Two overhead transparencies with grid lines on them (ask your teacher for them), or two clear plastic bags with grid lines drawn on them

---

» *Plant and Animal Kingdoms: Plants*, Denise Vega, Uechi Ng, and Kimberly King (Gareth Stevens, 2002)
» NASA: Kids science news network: Why do plants grow upwards? http://ksnn.larc.nasa.gov/webtext.cfm?unit=plants
» Adventures of the agronauts: Plants and gravity: http://www.ncsu.edu/project/agronauts/mission2_8.htm

Outline of methods

1. Soak the seeds in water overnight in the plastic cup.

2. Fill both sandwich bags with cotton wool balls.

3. Press the cotton wool balls down a bit. They will hold the sunflower seeds in place. The seeds will be spaced about 5 centimetres (2 inches) from each other.

Continued →

9

Step 6

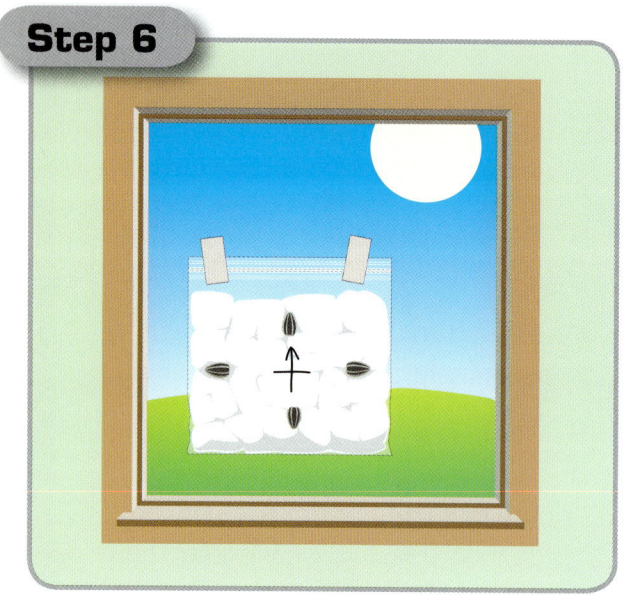

Step 9

4. To position the first four seeds, think of the bag as a compass. The pointed side of the first seed should face "north". The pointed end of the second seed should face "south", towards the bottom of the bag. The pointed side of the third seed should face "east", and the pointed side of the fourth seed should face "west".

5. Dampen the cotton wool balls so they are moist. Seal the sandwich bag, and then use the drawing pin to make several airholes in it.

6. Draw an arrow pointing up on the bag to show the original direction of the bag. Tape the bag to a sunny window.

7. Repeat steps 4 to 6 with the remaining sunflower seeds.

8. Observe and record the position of the root and the stem of each seed over several days. Check the moisture level in the cotton wool balls and add more water if they seem dry. Be careful not to disturb the position of the seeds.

9. Once the roots and stems are a few centimetres long, turn one of the bags upside down and re-tape it to the window. Tape the gridded overhead transparencies to both bags. Mark any changes in the direction of growth over several more days.

Analysis of results

» Did all four seeds in each bag grow in the same direction?

» Did the direction of growth change as the roots and stems continued to grow?

» What effect did turning the bag upside down have on the roots and stems?

More activities to extend your investigation

» Increase the number of bags of seeds used in this experiment. A larger sample will increase the accuracy of the results.

» Try using different types of seeds and compare their growth with that of the sunflower seeds.

» Turn grown plants upside down and compare the results with those you got with turning seeds upside down.

Project extras

» Include in your results the transparency grids you used to track the growth of each seed.

Cool seeds

Plants have **adapted** to grow in many environments around the world – from the hot savannas of Africa to the cold steppes of Asia. Plants need light to **germinate,** or begin to grow. But do they also need heat? Do seeds in cold areas grow at a slower rate than those in warmer temperatures? Try this experiment to find out.

Do your research

In this experiment, you will be growing grass seed. Before you get started, do some research on plants, grasses, and the effect temperature has on them. You'll also need to know about **fluorescent lights,** which emit light without heating up. Once you've done some research, you might try this project or one of your own. You will need to use a refrigerator for this project, so check with your parents before you start. You'll also need an adult to supervise setting up the lights.

You could start your research with this book and these websites:

» *DK Eyewitness: Plant,* David Burnie (Dorling Kindersley, 2004)
» Temperature effect on plants: http://www.ces.ncsu.edu/depts/hort/consumer/weather/tempeffect-plants.html
» How fluorescent lamps work:
http://home.howstuffworks.com/fluorescent-lamp.htm

Background information

Possible question

Does temperature affect the rate at which plants grow?

Possible hypothesis

Plants will grow more slowly at lower temperatures.

Level of difficulty

Advanced

Approximate cost of materials

£20.00

Materials needed

» Compass or other sharp tool
» 10 small paper or plastic cups
» Potting soil, enough to fill the 10 plastic cups

Materials needed (cont.)

» Grass seed, enough to evenly cover the soil in 10 small plastic cups (about 75–100 seeds per cup)
» Two plastic storage containers, each big enough to hold five plastic cups
» Two 45-centimetre (18-inch) fluorescent light bulbs and holders, or fluorescent light bulbs and fixtures from an old aquarium
» Two shoeboxes
» Refrigerator
» Two thermometers
» Two flat extension cables
» Large light-proof box, or a cupboard kept at room temperature
» Ruler
» Adult supervisor

Outline of methods

1. Use the compass to carefully poke a few holes in the bottom of each cup.

2. Fill each cup with potting soil to within 2 centimetres (¾ inch) of the top of the cup.

3. Spread the grass seeds in a single even layer over the potting soil in each cup.

4. Place five cups in each of the two plastic storage containers.

Continued

5. Pour half a cup of water into each cup. Leave the water that drains through the bottom in the storage container.

6. Place each storage container in a shoebox, and then place a fluorescent light on the top of each box. Make sure an adult helps you set up the fluorescent lights. It's also very important that you wash your hands after touching the soil.

ADULT SUPERVISION REQUIRED

Step 6

7. Put one box and light set-up in the refrigerator, along with one thermometer. Wait about five minutes for the thermometer to cool, and then record the temperature. Arrange the extension cable for the light so that the refrigerator door closes. If it won't close, try moving the cable along the refrigerator door until you find a place that allows the door to close.

8. Put the other thermometer, box, and light set-up in the light-proof box or in a room-temperature cupboard where sunlight cannot hit it. Record the temperature.

9. Observe the seeds twice a day. Add half a cup of water to each cup of seeds every three days. Record the day the grass germinates in each place. Once the grass begins to grow, use the ruler to measure the growth of five blades of grass in each cup. Then, record the average height of the grass in each cup.

10. Record the growth and temperature in each cup for several days. Compare the growth of the grass in both places.

Analysis of results

» Did the temperature remain constant in both places?
» Did the temperature affect the growth?
» Once the seeds germinated, did they grow at different rates because of the different temperatures?
» What other factors might have been involved?

More activities to extend your investigation

» Show the average height of the grass in the five cups in each place on your results table.
» Research the type of grass seed you used to find out in which climate it grows best.
» Try using two different types of grass seeds in this experiment.
» Extend the amount of time the grass grows in each place.
» Decrease the amount of time the plants are under the light. Then, note the difference in results from the original experiment.

Project extras

» Show the growth rate in both table and graph forms.
» Take photographs of your experiment so that you can show how the plants' growth changed.

Too much of a good thing?

Plants need **nutrients** to grow. Wild plants get nutrients on their own, but people add fertilisers to the plants grown in their homes and on farms. A recommended amount of fertiliser to be added to the plant is usually listed somewhere on the packet. But, if a little fertiliser is good, wouldn't a little more be better? Try this experiment to find out.

Do your research

You'll need at least a month and a lot of sunlight to complete this project. Make sure you give yourself enough time. You will be adding different amounts of fertiliser to radish plants. It is best to use a liquid fertiliser because it will be easy to vary the amount of fertiliser used while keeping it evenly distributed. Ask your parents about the best place to store the fertiliser to keep it away from pets and young children. Before you begin this project, do some research about plants and the nutrients they need to grow. Learn about fertilisers, too. Once you've done some research, you can begin the project described here or create your own unique project.

You could start your research with this book and these websites:

» *DK Eyewitness: Plant,* David Burnie (Dorling Kindersley, 2004)
» What you should know about fertilisers
   http://www.pda.org.uk/leaflets/25/no25-page1.htm
» Kids world: Plant nutrition
   http://www.agr.state.nc.us/cyber/kidswrld/plant/nutrient.htm

Background information

Possible question

Will increasing the amount of fertiliser improve a plant's growth?

Possible hypothesis

Plants will grow best with the recommended amount of fertiliser.

Level of difficulty

Advanced

Approximate cost of materials

£6.00

Materials needed

» Compass or other sharp tool
» 12 small paper or plastic cups
» Permanent marker pen
» Masking tape
» Potting soil, enough to fill eight small plastic cups
» 24 radish seeds
» Four plastic storage containers, each big enough to hold two small plastic cups
» Liquid house plant fertiliser, also known as plant food
» Four plastic bottles with lids, such as empty milk containers
» Ruler

Outline of methods

1. Use the compass to carefully poke a few holes in the bottom of eight of the plastic cups. Number the eight cups 1a and 1b, 2a and 2b, 3a and 3b, 4a and 4b. Add the following labels to the pairs of cups:
   a. 1a and 1b: water only
   b. 2a and 2b: recommended amount
   c. 3a and 3b: recommended amount x 1.5
   d. 4a and 4b: recommended amount x 2.0

2. Fill each cup with potting soil to within 2 centimetres (¾ inch) of the top of the cup. Place three radish seeds, evenly spaced, on the top of the soil in each cup. Gently cover each seed with a little soil.

3. Place one pair of the cups in each of the four plastic storage containers. Put all the containers in a sunny place.

 Continued

4. Label the remaining cups 1, 2, 3, and 4. You will use them to water the plants.

5. Label the four bottles the same way you labelled the cups.

6. Prepare a different fertiliser-and-water mixture in each of the plastic bottles. The first bottles contain only water; the second is made with the recommended amount of fertiliser; the third is made with 50 per cent more than the recommended amount; and the fourth is made with double the recommended amount.

7. Pour half a cup of water from bottle 1 into cup 1. Use this to water the seeds in the cups labelled 1a and 1b. Leave the water that drains through the bottom in the storage container.

8. Repeat step 7 using the mixtures in the other three bottles and the cups with matching labels.

9. Check the seeds daily. Water them with the corresponding fertiliser mixture according to the instructions given on the fertiliser container. Usually, this is once per week. If the soil is dry to the touch, add half a cup of tap water.

10. Record the first day on which at least one radish seed germinates in each cup. Once the radish plants begin to grow, use the ruler to measure the growth of three plants in each container, and average your results.

Step 10

Plant Growth

	Day 1	Day 2	Day 3	Day 4	Day 5
Water Only					
Cup 1a					
Seed 1			germinate	0.8 cm	1.6 cm
Seed 2				germinate	0.8 cm
Seed 3				germinate	1.0 cm
Cup 1b					
Seed 1				germinate	0.8 cm
Seed 2				germinate	0.7 cm
Seed 3					germinate
Recommended Amount					
Cup 2a					
Seed 1			germinate	1.1 cm	2.0 cm
Seed 2			germinate	1.1 cm	2.2 cm
Seed 2			germinate	1.4 cm	2.4 cm

11. Continue to add fertiliser and record the plant growth in each cup for several weeks. Compare the growth of the radishes from each set of cups.

Analysis of results

» Which set of plants grew the tallest?

» Which set grew the least?

» Did any of the plants have unusual or unexpected growth patterns?

» Is there a connection between the amount of fertiliser used and the amount of growth recorded?

More activities to extend your investigation

» Show the average height of the six radishes you grew in each container.

» Extend the amount of time you grow the radish plants to include growing a full radish. Measure the size of the radish grown with each fertiliser mixture.

» Use a different brand of fertiliser and note any differences in plant growth from what you observed in the original experiment.

» Research the ingredients of the fertiliser you used and describe their role in helping plants grow.

» Try the experiment using water plants, such as duckweed, instead of using plants that grow in soil. See whether the water plants are affected by fertiliser in the same way as the soil-grown plants.

Project extras

» Show the growth of the radishes in both table and graph forms.

So long, starch

Leaves are a plant's manufacturing site. They are where sunlight, water, and carbon dioxide are used to make food for the plant in the form of starches and sugars. This process is called **photosynthesis.** Will a leaf continue to produce starch once sunlight is taken away? This project will let you find out.

Do your research

In this experiment you'll be using iodine, which you might find in your medicine cabinet. Make sure you keep it away from young children and pets. You will also need to boil leaves in water. Wear safety goggles and make sure an adult is present when you are working with any heating device.

You'll need several large geranium leaves and a full day of sunlight. You'll be cutting the leaves off the plant, so make sure you ask for permission to do so. Before you begin, do some research on photosynthesis to find out more about starch production. You should also learn about iodine and its reaction to starch. Then, you'll be ready to try this project. Or, your research may lead you to try something else.

Here is a book and a website you could start with in your research:

» *The Green World: Photosynthesis and Respiration*, William G Hopkins (Chelsea House, 2006)

» Photosynthesis: http://kent.skoool.co.uk/content/keystage3/biology/pc/ learningsteps/ROPLC/launch.html

Background information

Possible question

What will happen to starch production if a leaf is removed from sunlight?

Possible hypothesis

Starch production will stop after a few hours without sunlight.

Level of difficulty

Advanced

Approximate cost of materials

£7.00

Materials needed

» 12 geranium leaves
» 10 pieces of aluminium foil, each about 5 centimetres x 10 centimetres (2 inches x 4 inches)

Materials needed (cont.)

» 10 paper clips
» Scissors
» Six plastic trays or plates
» Permanent marker pen
» Masking tape
» Safety goggles
» Hot plate
» Isopropyl alcohol (You may be able to buy this from a pharmacy or from an electrical shop).
» Two saucepans (One should be able to fit inside the other.)
» Water
» Oven gloves
» Metal tongs
» Iodine
» Eyedropper or pipette
» Kitchen towel
» Adult supervisor

Outline of methods

1. Choose 10 leaves on the geranium plant that are well exposed to sunlight. Fold a piece of aluminium foil over each leaf so it is completely covered. Use the paper clips to hold the foil in place.

2. Immediately after clipping the foil in place, cut two leaves that have not been covered by aluminium foil.

Continued

3. Label the six plastic trays to correspond with the time you will be checking the leaves for starch:

    a. Test 1: Control
    b. Test 2: 2 hours
    c. Test 3: 4 hours
    d. Test 4: 6 hours
    e. Test 5: 8 hours
    f. Test 6: 24 hours

Step 4

4. Put on your safety goggles. With adult supervision, warm 100 millilitres (3.3 fluid ounces) of alcohol in the small pan, which should sit over the water-filled larger pan. Use oven gloves to carefully put the pot of warmed alcohol to one side. **Caution: Alcohol is flammable. Never heat using an open flame.**

ADULT SUPERVISION REQUIRED

5. Return the large pan of water to the boil.

6. Place the two cut leaves in the boiling water for five minutes. Boiling breaks down the leaf's cell walls.

Step 7

7. Use the metal tongs to move the leaves from the boiling water into the alcohol for two minutes. The alcohol removes the chlorophyll from the leaf. This is done so you can clearly see the iodine-starch reaction.

8. Place the leaves on a piece of kitchen towel and pat them dry. Then, transfer the leaves to the tray labelled Test 1: Control.

9. Use the eyedropper or pipette to put two or three drops of iodine on each leaf. Observe the leaves for one minute. The iodine should change colour from orange to blue-black or purple as it reacts to starch in the leaves.

10. After two hours, boil water and heat the alcohol as directed in steps 4 and 5. Then, cut off two of the foil-covered leaves and repeat steps 6 to 9. Record your results.

11. Continue the procedure in step 9 for Tests 3 to 6 at the times listed. Compare the iodine colour from each test.

12. Put the lid tightly on the iodine bottle and ask an adult to put it away. The used alcohol can go down the sink. Wrap the leaves in kitchen towel before throwing them in the bin.

Analysis of results

» Did all the leaves cause the iodine to turn purple?
» Did the iodine not react on any of the leaves?
» Were there differences in the colour changes?

More activities to extend your investigation

» Research plant sources of starch in human diets.
» Try using leaves from different plants and compare their reaction time with that of the geranium leaves.
» Try the same experiment again at a different time of year. Compare the results with those from the original experiment.

Project extras

» Include photographs of the leaves before the iodine is added.
» Include photographs of the leaves after the iodine reacted to starch.
» Make a diagram showing the process of photosynthesis to include in your report.

Just add water

Seeds need the right conditions to begin growing. One important factor is water – without it, seeds cannot grow. How much water can seeds absorb? Is the amount of water related to a seed's size? You can find out by trying this experiment.

Do your research

Water is the first trigger for **germination,** the process in which seeds begin to grow. Before you begin this project, do some research on germination and seeds. Once you've done some research, you'll be ready to dig into this project. Or, you may come up with your own unique project after you've read and learned more about the topic.

Here are some books and websites you could start with in your research:

» *World of Plants: Seeds,* John Farndon (Blackbirch Press, 2006)
» *The Green World: Plant Development*, William G Hopkins (Chelsea House, 2006)
» Great plant escape: Germination
   http://www.urbanext.uiuc.edu/gpe/case3/c3facts3.html
» Biology of plants: Starting to grow: http://mbgnet.net/bioplants/grow.html

Background information

Possible question

Does a seed's size and shape affect the amount of water it can absorb?

Possible hypothesis

Seeds that are big and thick can absorb more water than seeds of other sizes.

Level of difficulty

Easy

Approximate cost of materials

£4.00

Materials needed

» Kitchen scales
» 10 pea seeds of similar size
» Four medium-sized plastic cups
» Water
» 10 kidney bean seeds of similar size
» 10 broad bean seeds of similar size
» 10 pumpkin seeds of similar size
» Kitchen towel

Outline of methods

1. Place 10 pea seeds on the scales.

2. Weigh the pea seeds. Find the average weight of one pea seed by dividing by 10. Record your results.

3. Put the pea seeds in a plastic cup and fill the cup with enough water to completely cover all the seeds.

4. Repeat steps 1, 2, and 3 with the kidney bean, broad bean, and pumpkin seeds. Let all the seeds soak for 24 hours.

 Continued

Step 5

5. Before weighing the soaked kidney bean seeds, you'll need to get rid of any excess water that wasn't absorbed by the seeds. Gently remove the seeds from the cup and pat them dry with kitchen towel. Then, weigh the soaked seeds. Find the average weight of one kidney bean seed by dividing by 10. Record your results.

6. Repeat step 5 for the other three types of seeds.

7. Find the percentage weight gain using this formula: Subtract the original weight from the new weight. Divide the difference by the original weight. Convert the result to a percentage by moving the decimal point two places to the right.

8. Compare the percentage weight gain of all four types of seeds.

Step 7

10 pumpkin seeds dry weight:
4 grams/10 seeds = 0.4g/seed

10 pumpkin seeds soaked weight:
9 grams/10 seeds = 0.9g/seed

0.9 - 0.4 = 0.5
0.5/0.4 = 1.25
1.25 = 125%

Analysis of results

» Did all four seed types absorb the same amount of water?

» If not, which seed absorbed the most water? Which absorbed the least?

» Rank the seeds according to the percentage of water absorbed. Did one seed absorb a greater percentage of water than the others? Was the percentage of water absorbed related to the original weight of the seed?

More activities to extend your investigation

» Research seed banks and how seeds are stored in them. Seeds can remain **viable** for years if they are kept in a dry environment.

» Try using different types of seeds in this experiment.

» Compare the amount of water each type of seed absorbed after one hour. Did the seed that absorbed the most water after one hour absorb the most water overall?

Project extras

» Show your results in both table and graph forms.

» Take photographs of each seed type before and after soaking.

Colour my world

Light is essential for plant growth. Sunlight is the main light source for plants on Earth. You may know that sunlight is actually made up of different colours. But is any single colour best for plant growth? Try this experiment and find out.

Do your research

This project will take at least a month to complete, so make sure you give yourself enough time. Sunlight is made from a rainbow of light colours. Plants use sunlight to make food in a process called photosynthesis. Before you begin this project, do some research on photosynthesis and sunlight. Once you've done some research, you can tackle this project. Or, you may come up with your own unique project after you've learned more.

You could start your research with this book and these websites:

» *Photosynthesis: Changing Sunlight Into Food*, Bobbie Kalman (Crabtree Publishing, 2005)

» Photosynthesis and transpiration (made easy): http://www.cornwallwildlifetrust.org.uk/educate/kids/photsyn.htm

» Photosynthesis: http://www.bbc.co.uk/schools/gcsebitesize/biology/greenplantsasorganisms/Ophotosynthesisrev1.shtml

Background information

Possible question

Does the colour of light affect plant growth?

Possible hypothesis

Plants grown in coloured light will not grow as quickly as plants grown in normal sunlight.

Level of difficulty

Intermediate

Approximate cost of materials

£7.00

Materials needed

» Five 2-litre drinks bottles with lids
» Scissors
» Red, green, blue, yellow, and clear cellophane, enough of each to completely cover a 2-litre bottle
» Clear sticky tape
» Gravel, enough to make a thin layer in the bottom of five 2-litre bottles
» Potting soil, enough to fill the bottom of five 2-litre bottles to a depth of 5 centimetres (2 inches)
» 25 broad bean seeds
» Water
» Ruler
» Adult supervisor

Outline of methods

1. Remove the labels from the 2-litre bottles. Cut each bottle apart about 9 centimetres (3½ inches) from the bottom. Then, cut six 1.25-centimetre (½-inch) slits along the rim of the bottom so the top portion of the bottle can fit over it. Make sure an adult helps you cut the bottles. Trim any jagged edges.

Step 1

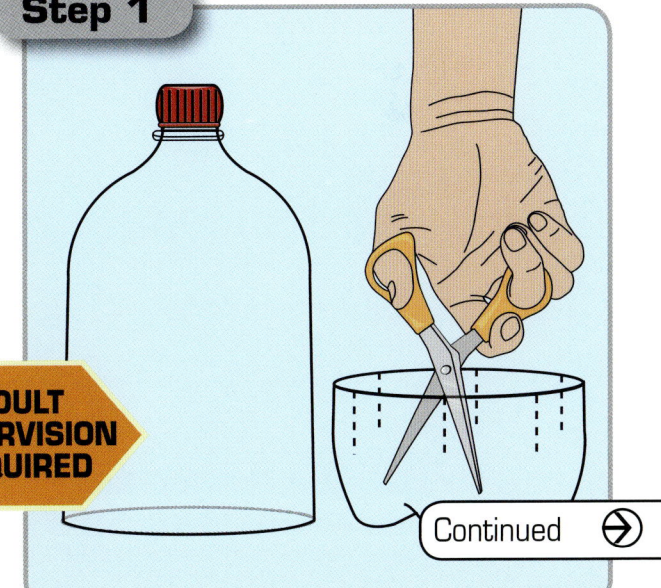

ADULT SUPERVISION REQUIRED

Continued ➔

2. Cover the top of each bottle with a different colour of cellophane. Use clear cellophane for growing the control group of seeds. Attach the cellophane to the bottle top with clear sticky tape.

3. Spread a thin layer of gravel in the base of each bottle for drainage and to give the base extra weight. Then, add a layer of potting soil about 5 centimetres (2 inches) deep.

4. Gently push five broad bean seeds into the soil along the sides of each base so you can still see them through the plastic.

5. Add water to the soil so that it is damp. Make sure you add the same amount of water to all five bases.

6. Cover each base with one of the tops that are now covered with cellophane, to make **terrariums.** Put all five terrariums in a sunny place. Do not add water; the terrariums should stay moist. Avoid exposing the plants to non-filtered sunlight during the experiment.

Step 6

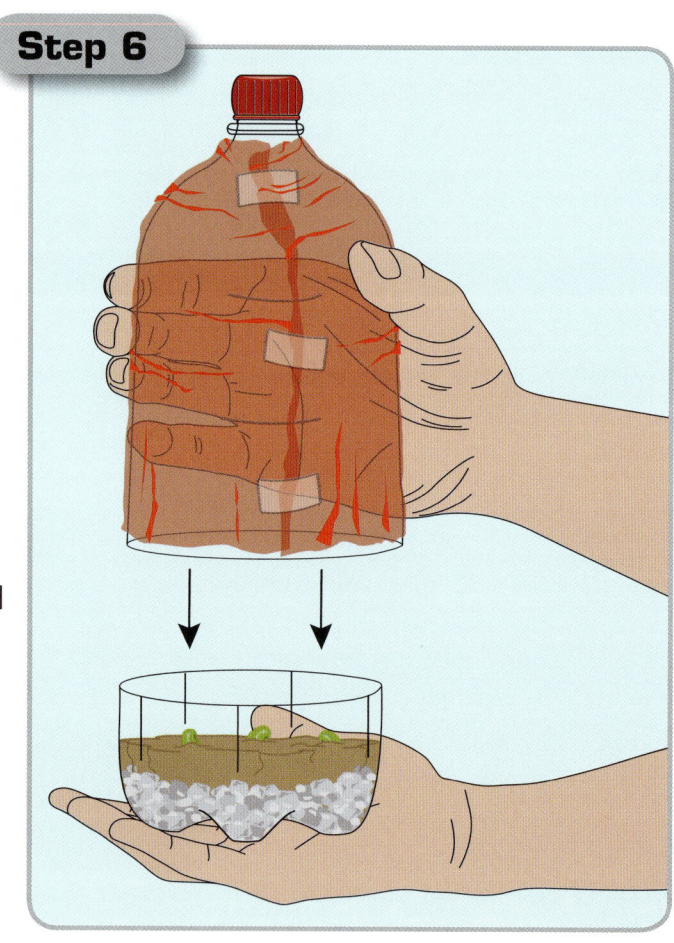

7. Observe and record the growth of the seeds in each terrarium over several weeks. Compare the growth in the terrariums.

Analysis of results

» Did all of the broad bean seeds in each terrarium germinate at the same time?

» Was there a difference in the growth rates from one terrarium to the next?

» Did all the broad beans in each terrarium grow at the same rate?

More activities to extend your investigation

» Increase the number of seeds in each terrarium. More information increases the accuracy of the results.

» Try using other colours of cellophane, such as purple and orange.

» Experiment with other kinds of seeds and compare their growth with that of the broad bean seeds.

Project extras

» Show your results in both table and graph forms. The colours of your graphs could match the colours of the cellophane.

» Create artwork that shows light breaking into its range of colours as it goes through a prism. Add the rainbow prism art to your investigation report.

Stem straws

Plant stems have many functions. Stems hold up the flower and store food for the plant, and they also transport water and nutrients. If the water is in the ground, how does a stem seem to defy gravity to bring the water to the top of the plant? How quickly does this happen? Do different plants move water at different rates? You can find the answers to these questions with this project.

Do your research

Stems have specialised cells called **xylem** that transport water. Water movement is due to a process called **transpiration,** in which water is transported from the stem's xylem cells to the leaves, where the water **evaporates.** Before you begin this project, do some research on stems and how water moves through a plant. Then, you can tackle this project or come up with your own unique project after you've read and learned more about the topic.

Here are some books and websites you could start with in your research:

» *Plant Parts: Stems*, Vijaya Bodach (Pebble Plus, 2006)
» *World of Plants: Stems*, John Farndon (Blackbirch Press, 2006)

Background information

Possible question

Do different flowering plants move water at different rates?

Possible hypothesis

Plants with thicker stems will move the water more quickly.

Level of difficulty

Easy

Approximate cost of materials

£10.00

Materials needed

» Two long-stemmed white roses
» Two long-stemmed white daisies
» Two long-stemmed white carnations
» Two long-stemmed white lilies
» 2-litre (4.2-pint) container
» Measuring jug or graduated cylinder
» Red food colouring
» Eight ½-litre (1-pint) plastic bottles
» Tape measure
» Scissors

» Stems: http://www.mcwdn.org/Plants/Stems.html
» Plant nutrition: http://lgfl.skoool.co.uk/examcentre.aspx?id=256

Outline of methods

1. While you are preparing your materials, keep your flowers in a container of water. Do your measuring and cutting as quickly as possible to avoid letting air into the bottom of the stems.

2. Mix 2 litres (4.2 pints) of water with 100 drops of red food colouring (approximately one small bottle of food colouring).

3. Pour 50 millilitres (0.1 pint) of the red water into each of the eight ½-litre (1-pint) plastic bottles.

Continued

4. Use the tape measure to find the flower with the shortest stem. Cut each stem at an angle about 2.5 centimetres (1 inch) above this length, so that the length of each flower's stem is equal to that of the others. Quickly place each flower into one of the ½-litre (1-pint) bottles.

5. Keep the pieces of stem that you cut off. Measure each stem's diameter by standing the stem on its end and tracing it on a sheet of blank paper.

6. Record the time at the beginning of the experiment.

7. Observe and record the colour of the flowers every 15 minutes. You will know the water has moved from the base of the stem into the flower when the flower begins to look red.

8. Continue your observations until all the flowers look a reddish colour.

Step 7

Flower type:
Carnation #1
Diameter: 4mm

Date: 20/9
Start Time: 4:00 pm
15 min:
30 min:
45 min:
End time:

Amount of water absorbed

Analysis of results

» Did all four types of flowers turn red at the same time?

» If not, in what order did they change colour?

» Did the diameter of the stems have any bearing on the rate that the water moved up them?

» What other factors might be involved? For example, did any stem have leaves on it? Were all the stems green or were some woody?

More activities to extend your investigation

» After the first flower becomes red, remove one of each type of flower from its container. Then, measure the amount of water that remains in each container. The flower whose container has the least amount of water remaining moved the most water.

» Identify other factors that may have affected your results, such as the size of the flower or the number of leaves on the stem.

» Use a fan to create a breeze near the flowers. Observe whether moving air changes the results of your experiment.

» Try the experiment using celery stems with leaves instead of flowers. Investigate which factors affect the rate that the water moves, such as temperature or the amount of light the plants receive.

Project extras

» Include "before" and "after" photographs of your flowers as part of your report.

» Show your results in both table and graph forms.

Undercover colour

Many leaves change colour in autumn, going from dark green to brilliant reds, yellows, and oranges. Where do these colours come from, and where does the green colour go? Find out about leaf colours with this project.

Do your research

To prepare the leaves, you'll be crushing them in acetone (the chemical found in nail varnish remover) and leaving them in the solution overnight. As with any chemical, keep acetone away from small children and pets. Wear safety goggles to protect your eyes during this procedure.

The green colour of leaves is due to **chlorophyll,** a chemical necessary for photosynthesis to occur. The other colours are natural pigments in the leaf that are most prominent as the plant is ready to lie dormant for the winter months. It is best to do this project in late summer or early autumn, just before the leaves begin to change colour. You will then need to wait until the leaves do change so that you can compare the colours in your experiment with the colours of the autumn leaves. Make sure you time your project to include the colour change.

Before you begin, do some research on autumn leaves and **chromatography,** the process you'll use in this experiment to determine the autumn leaf colours. Once you've done some research, you can try this project or come up with your own unique project.

Background information

Possible question

Can the autumn colour of a leaf be determined before it changes colour?

Possible hypothesis

Colours can be determined by removing the chlorophyll from the leaf.

Level of difficulty

Easy

Approximate cost of materials

£3.00

Materials needed

» Two leaves from each of four different trees, such as rowan, poplar, beech, oak, or elm
» Safety goggles
» Pestle and mortar, or another way to mash up the leaves, such as a spoon and bowl made of heavy plastic
» Four test tubes and a test tube holder, or four clear plastic cups
» Acetone (nail varnish remover)
» Two white coffee filters
» Scissors
» Four pencils
» Sticky tape
» Plastic container for waste disposal

Here are some books and websites you could start with in your research:

» *Plant Parts: Leaves*, Vijaya Bodach (Capstone Press, 2006)
» *World of Plants: Leaves*, John Farndon (Blackbirch Press, 2006)
» Why do leaves change colour in autumn?:
http://www.cornwallwildlifetrust.org.uk/educate/kids/leaves.htm
» Chromatography:
http://acs.chem.ku.edu/Carnival2001/Activities/chromatography.asp

Continued

Outline of methods

1. Ask for permission to select a few leaves from trees before you begin collecting them. Note the location of the trees you are using for this project so you can check the colour of their leaves in autumn.

2. Collect at least four varieties of leaves. You'll need two leaves of each type. Put on your safety goggles, and then mash up each pair of leaves with the pestle and mortar. Place one pair of mashed-up leaves in each test tube.

3. Cover the leaf mash with acetone. Leave the mixture for 24 hours.

4. Prepare the coffee filters for the chromatography. Cut four strips from the coffee filters, each should be 1.25 centimetres (½ inch) wide. Cut the bottom of the strip to form a point. Place one strip in each test tube so that the pointed end is just touching the acetone/leaf mixture. Tape the other end of each strip to a pencil and put the pencil across the top of the test tube.

5. Observe the filter strips every 30 minutes for two hours and record your results. Take a final observation after 24 hours and record any changes. The strip in each test tube should have a green line, followed by one or more lines of different colours.

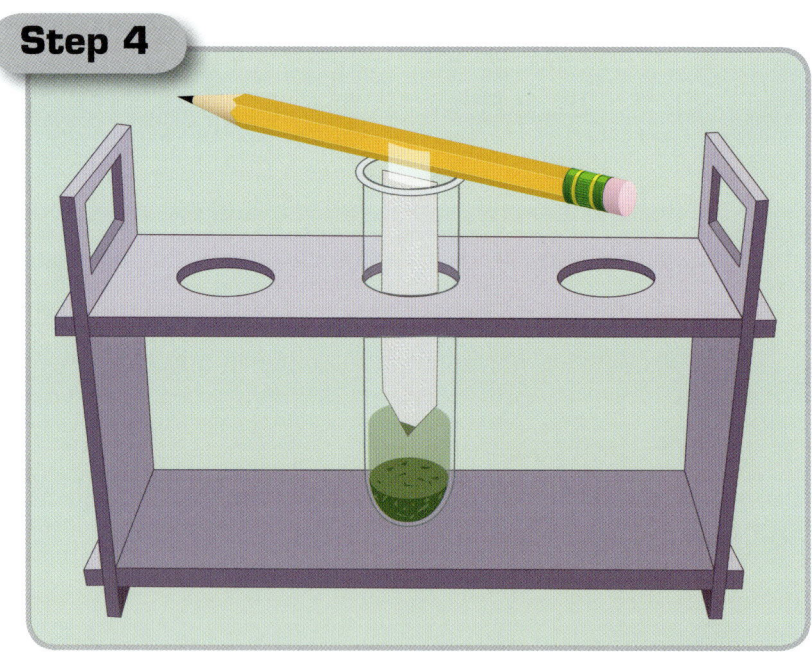

Step 4

6. When you have finished with your observations, put the acetone/leaf mixture into a plastic container, such as an empty ice cream tub, and dispose of it as hazardous waste. Contact your local council to find out how to do this in your area.

7. Compare these colours to the colour of the leaves from the same tree in autumn.

Analysis of results

» Did the filter strips stay white?

» If not, what colours did you see on the strips?

» Did the leaf colours match the autumn colours of the leaves from the same tree?

More activities to extend your investigation

» Research the way in which chlorophyll is changed in leaves during autumn.

» Make a chart showing the average dates for autumn colour changes in your area.

» Try chromatography on leaves from several other trees or leaves from non-woody plants.

Project extras

» Include the paper chromatography strips in your report.

» Include drawings of both summer and autumn leaves of each type of tree you used in your experiment.

» Include photos of the trees in summer and in autumn, after their leaves change colour.

» Make a chart showing the annual life cycle of a tree.

Microwave manipulation

Microwaves are part of our everyday life. We use microwaves to heat our food, send and receive messages, even guide aeroplanes. Microwave **radiation** is detected everywhere in the universe. So how does all this radiation affect plant growth? What will happen to seeds when they are exposed to microwaves from a microwave oven?

Do your research

This project requires at least four weeks to finish. Make sure you have planned enough time to complete it. You'll also need an adult to approve the use of the microwave and to supervise you when you are heating seeds. Before you begin this project, do some research to find out more about plants and different types of microwave radiation. Then, you can try this project or you may come up with your own version.

Here are some books and websites you could start with in your research:

» *The Green World: Plant Development*, William G Hopkins (Chelsea House, 2006)
» *Life Science In Depth: Green Plants*, Sally Morgan (Heinemann, 2006)
» NASA: Microwave effects on plant growth:
   http://www.nasa.gov/centers/ames/news/releases/2003/03_94AR.html
» What are microwaves?
   http://www.ieee-virtual-museum.org/exhibit/exhibit.php?id=159265&lid=1

Background information

Possible question

Does microwave radiation affect the growth of plants?

Possible hypothesis

Plant growth will be affected by radiation from a microwave oven.

Level of difficulty

Advanced

Approximate cost of materials

£9.00

Materials needed

» 100 marigold seeds
» Plastic cup
» 100 4-centimetre (1.5-inch) peat pots (These biodegradable pots are available from a garden centre.)
» Permanent marker pen
» Potting soil, enough to fill 100 peat pots
» Four plastic trays, each large enough to hold 25 peat pots
» Measuring jug
» Kitchen towel
» Microwave oven
» Adult supervisor

Outline of methods

1. Soak all of the seeds in water overnight in the plastic cup.
2. While you are soaking the seeds, label the peat pots as follows:
   a. Label 25 pots M-10 for "microwaved 10 seconds".
   b. Label 25 pots M-20 for "microwaved 20 seconds".
   c. Label 25 pots M-30 for "microwaved 30 seconds".
   d. Label 25 pots M-0 for "microwaved 0 seconds". This will be your control group.
3. Fill all of the peat pots with potting soil. Plant the 25 control seeds in the M-0 pots according to the directions on the seed packet. Place the pots on one of the four plastic trays; water each pot with about 50 millilitres (1.7 fluid ounces) of water. Leave the water that drains through in the tray.

Continued

4. You are now ready to microwave the rest of the seeds. With an adult supervising, place 25 seeds on kitchen towel in the microwave. Microwave the seeds at full power for 10 seconds, and then plant them in the M-10 peat pots. Place the pots on a tray; water as you did for the control group.

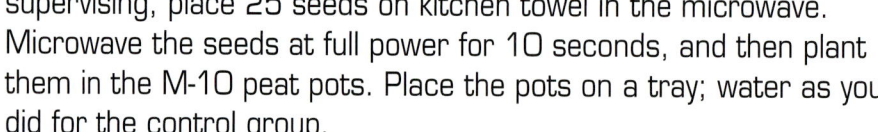

Step 4

5. Repeat step 4 with 25 new seeds, but microwave them for 20 seconds and plant them in the pots labelled M-20.

6. Repeat step 4 with the remaining 25 seeds, but microwave them for 30 seconds and plant them in the pots labelled M-30.

7. Place all of the trays in a sunny place. Water the pots with the same amount of water when the soil is dry to the touch.

8. Record the date that each seed germinates. After two weeks, record the total number of seeds that germinated from each group.

Analysis of results

» Did all of the seeds germinate?
» If not, which group of seeds had the greatest number of germinated seeds?
» Which group germinated in the least amount of time?
» Which group took longest to germinate?

More activities to extend your investigation

» Continue the experiment to determine whether microwave radiation affects the growth of the marigold plants.
» Try using different types of seeds and compare the effect of radiation with the effect on the marigold seeds.
» Double the amount of time each seed is microwaved. Be careful: The seeds might get very hot. Compare the results with those of your original experiment.
» Test what would happen if the seeds were exposed to other forms of radiation. For example, you could ask your dentist to let you put some seeds on top of your lead apron the next time you get your teeth X-rayed!

Project extras

» Show your results in both graph and table forms.
» Take photographs of your peat pots at regular intervals to show which seeds have germinated in which groups.

Writing your report

In many ways, writing the report of your investigation is the hardest part. You've researched the science involved, and you've had fun gathering all your evidence together. Now you have to explain what it's all about.

You are the expert

Very few other people, if any, will have done your investigation. So you are the expert here. You need to explain your ideas clearly. Scientists get their most important investigations published in a scientific magazine or journal. They may also stand up at meetings and tell other scientists what they have found. Or they may display a large poster to explain their investigation. You might consider giving a talk or making a poster about your investigation, too. But however scientists present their investigations, they always write it down first – and you must too. Here are some tips about what you should include in your report.

Some hints for collecting your results

» **Making a table:** Tables are great for recording lots of results. Use a pencil and ruler to draw your table lines, or make a table using a word processing program. Put the units (m, s, kg, N and so on) in the headings only. Don't write them into the main body of your table. Try to make your table fit one side of paper. If you need two sheets of paper, make sure you write the column headings on the second sheet as well.

» **Recording your results:** It is often easy to forget to write down your results as they come in. Or you might just scribble them onto the back of your hand, and then wash your hands! A wise scientist will always make a neat, blank table in their lab book before starting. They will write down their results as they go along and not later on.

» **Odd stuff:** If something goes wrong, make a note of it. This will remind you which results might not be reliable.

» **Precision:** Always record your readings to the precision of your measuring equipment. For example, if you have scales that show 24.6 g, don't write 24 or 25 in your table. Instead, write 24.6 because that's the precise measurement.

Laying out your report

You could use the following headings to organise your report in a clear manner:

» **A title**
This gives an idea of what your investigation is about.

» **Aims**
Write a brief outline of what you were trying to do. It should include the question you were trying to answer.

» **Hypothesis**
This is your scientific prediction of what will happen in your investigation. Include notes from your research to explain why you think your prediction will work out. It might help to write it out as: "I think … will happen because …"

» **Materials**
List the equipment you used to carry out your experiments. Also say what any measuring equipment was for. For example, "scales (to weigh the objects)".

» **Methods**
Explain what you actually did in your investigation.

» **Results**
Record your results, readings, and observations clearly.

» **Conclusions**
Explain how closely your results fitted your hypothesis. You can find out more about this on the next page.

» **Bibliography**
List the books, articles, websites or other resources you used in your research.

And finally ... the conclusions

There are two main bits to your conclusions. These are the "Analysis" and the "Evaluation". In the analysis you explain what your evidence shows, and how it supports or disproves your hypothesis. In the evaluation, you discuss the quality of your results and their reliability, and how successful your methods were.

Your analysis

You need to study your evidence to see if there is a relationship between the variables in your investigation. This can be difficult to spot in a table, so it is a good idea to draw a graph. You should always put the dependent variable on the vertical axis, and the independent variable on the horizontal axis. The type of graph you need to draw depends on the type of variables involved:

» A bar chart if the results are **categoric**, such as hot/cold, male/female.
» A line graph or a scattergram if both variables are **continuous**, such as time, length, or mass.

Remember to label the axes to say what each one shows, and the unit used. For example, "time in s" or "height in cm". Draw a line or curve of best fit if you can.

Explain what your graph shows. Remember that the reader needs help from you to understand your investigation. Even if you have spotted a pattern, don't assume that your reader has. Tell them. For example, "My graph shows that the more fertiliser used, the bigger the plant grew". Circle any points on your graph that seem anomalous (too high or too low).

Your evaluation

Did your investigation go well, or did it go badly? Was your evidence good enough for you to support or disprove your hypothesis? Sometimes it can be difficult for you to answer these questions. But it is really important that you try. Scientists always look back at their investigations. They want to know if they could improve their methods next time. They also want to know if their evidence is reliable and valid. Reliable evidence can be repeated with pretty much the same results. Valid evidence is reliable, and it should answer the question you asked in the first place. As before, remember that you are the person who knows your investigation the best. Don't be afraid to show off valid evidence. And be honest if it's not!

Glossary

accurate close to the true value

adapted changed in order to be suitable to live under specific conditions

categoric variable that can be given labels, such as male/female

chlorophyll green colouring in plants that is necessary for photosynthesis

chromatography technique for separating materials

continuous variable that can have any value, such as weight or length

control something that is left unchanged in order to compare results against it

data factual information

evaporates changes from a liquid into a vapour or gas

evidence data that has been checked to see if it is valid

fluorescent light glass tube in which light is produced by gases that react to an electric current

geotropism growth in response to gravity

germinate begin to grow; sprout

germination first stage in the development of a seed into a plant

hypothesis scientific idea about how something works, before the idea has been tested

nutrients chemicals that plants and animals need for growth and development

photosynthesis process in green plants in which carbon dioxide, water, and sunlight are used to create nutrients for the plant

prediction say in advance what you think will happen, based on scientific study

radiation energy output in the form of waves or rays

terrarium closed container used for growing plants

transpiration process in which plants lose water

tropism reaction of a plant due to external stimuli, such as light or gravity

variable something that can change; is not set or fixed

viable able to live

xylem tissue found in some plants for transporting water

Index